DISCOVER
STATELY HOMES
FROM ABOVE

The impressive east and south sides of Wilton House, Wiltshire

JOHN MANNION

MYRIAD
LONDON

BUCKINGHAM PALACE, LONDON *above*

BUCKINGHAM PALACE was built by John Sheffield, the Duke of Buckingham, in 1703. In 1762 George III bought the house (for £28,000) for his wife Charlotte and renamed it Queen's House. It was George IV who turned the house into Buckingham Palace. The architect John Nash faced the exterior with Bath stone, demolished and rebuilt the north and south wings and added new rooms on the western side. Nash ran hopelessly over budget and there were arguments over style. He designed Marble Arch as the grand entrance to the courtyard but was overruled. George IV died before work was finished and Nash was replaced by Edward Blore, who completed the work by adding a fourth wing and turning the Palace into a quadrangle in the 1830s. It was only in 1837, with the accession of Queen Victoria, that Buckingham Palace became the official residence of the British monarchy.

Today the palace has over 600 rooms, although the Queen and Duke of Edinburgh occupy only 12 of them.

✳

SYON PARK, BRENTFORD *left*

SYON HOUSE is the London home of the Dukes of Northumberland. It is built on the site of a medieval abbey and has witnessed numerous turbulent events. The father confessor to the abbey refused Henry VIII's new religion and was martyred. Henry VIII's coffin, en route to Windsor for burial, split open at Syon House and dogs chewed at his remains. Lady Jane Grey accepted the crown that was to lead to her execution at Syon House and the 9th Earl of Northumberland spent 15 years in prison because of a meeting at Syon House with one of the Gunpowder plot conspirators.

HAMPTON COURT, SURREY *above*

BUILDING AT HAMPTON COURT BEGAN in 1514 under the auspices of Thomas Wolsey, then Archbishop of York. The first version of the palace was accounted a wonder by contemporaries and, perhaps in fear that it outshone King Henry VIII's palaces at St James's and Whitehall, Wolsey gave it to Henry in exchange for Richmond Palace.

Henry re-modelled Wolsey's designs and produced one of the most sophisticated and opulent palaces of the period which included tennis courts, bowling alleys, pleasure gardens, a hunting park, huge kitchens, a fine chapel, a Great Hall and a lavatory which could sit 28 people at a time.

Hampton Court remained popular as a royal residence until the reign of George III, who preferred Windsor Castle; although it did see duty as a prison shortly after the Civil War. Extensive rebuilding was undertaken by Sir Christopher Wren but after the palace stopped being a royal residence the tendency has been to restore the building to its original Tudor glory.

WOBURN ABBEY, BEDFORDSHIRE *left*

WOBURN ABBEY was given to Sir John Russell for services to King Henry VIII in 1547 and became the family seat of the Russell family in 1619. Today's Woburn Abbey dates from 1747 when it was partially reconstructed and extended by the Palladian architect Henry Flitcroft. Further rebuilding took place in 1786 under the direction of Henry Holland. Although some of his work had to be demolished in 1949 his influence remains in the Venetian room and library.

Woburn's 3,000-acre deer park was landscaped by Humphry Repton in the early 19th century. One species of deer, the Pere David, is descended from the imperial herd of China and was saved from extinction at Woburn.

Woburn houses extensive collections of furniture, porcelain, silver and paintings. Works by Claude, Cuyp, Gainsborough, Murillo, Rembrandt and Reynolds are on display. The Venetian Room has 21 paintings of Venice by Canaletto.

✳

WINDSOR CASTLE, BERKSHIRE *below*

BUILT BY WILLIAM THE CONQUEROR and still going strong, Windsor Castle is one of the largest inhabited castles in the world. The Round Tower and the original stone outer walls were constructed by Henry II. St George's Chapel was started in 1475 by Edward IV and was completed in 1525 by Henry VIII. It is a fine example of late medieval perpendicular Gothic architecture and is the burial place of 10 English monarchs. Following the Civil War the castle was increasingly used as a royal palace and various alterations have been made over the years to improve its level of comfort. The castle today is much as it was in the early 19th century. It is an official Royal residence and the lavishly decorated state apartments are still used for state and official functions. Works of art by Canaletto, Holbein, Leonardo da Vinci, Rembrandt, Rubens and Van Dyck are on display there.

CLIVEDEN, BUCKINGHAMSHIRE *above*

THE CURRENT CLIVEDEN HOUSE is the third on the site. The architect Charles Barry, designer of the Houses of Parliament, was commissioned to rebuild Cliveden after a fire in 1849 and created today's Italianate villa. The 100 ft (30m) tall Water Tower is the work of Henry Clutton and the gardens were designed by John Fleming. Fleming's parterre can still be seen as can the swards of bluebells that he planted in the nearby woods.

Cliveden has always been more famous for its visitors than for its architecture and the house, now appropriately a hotel, has played host to numerous English kings and queens. In 1893 the house was purchased by William Waldorf Astor, the Bill Gates of his day, and in 1906 became the home of Nancy Astor, the first woman MP. Cliveden was at the centre of Nancy Astor's social life and her guests included Charlie Chaplin, Winston Churchill, President Roosevelt, George Bernard Shaw and Harold Macmillan.

AUDLEY END, ESSEX *left*

THOMAS, FIRST EARL OF SUFFOLK commissioned Audley End House to impress James I, but with little success as Suffolk fell out of favour in 1620 just as the house was being completed. It has had a chequered history ever since.

In 1668 Charles II bought the house to use as a base when visiting the races at Newmarket. By the 1680s it was in need of major repairs and William III returned Audley End to the Suffolk family.

Further decline followed until 1745 when it was purchased for the heir to the Countess of Portsmouth. A suite of neo-classical rooms and a Gothic chapel designed by Robert Adam were added and Capability Brown was employed to remodel the grounds.

The interior of the house reflects the ownership by the third Baron Braybrooke who was a great collector of pictures and furniture. The fourth Baron Braybrooke collected natural history specimens. After requisitioning during the Second World War, Audley End was sold to the Ministry of Works in 1948.

STRATFIELD SAYE HOUSE, HAMPSHIRE *left*

STRATFIELD SAYE HOUSE has been the home of the Dukes of Wellington since 1817. The main part of the house and stable blocks were built around 1630 by Sir William Pitt, James I's Comptroller of the Household. In the 18th century the red brick was faced in white stucco but this has since been removed.

When Arthur Wellesley, the 1st Duke of Wellington, bought the property in 1817 he planned to pull down the house and replace it with a grand "Waterloo Palace" but these plans were eventually abandoned on the grounds of expense. Instead the existing house was remodelled and improved. A conservatory was added in 1838 and outer wings in 1846. Wellesley also introduced central heating and two of the original radiators can still be seen.

One of the features of the gardens is Copenhagen's grave. Copenhagen was the horse that carried the Duke of Wellington through the Peninsular campaigns and the battle of Waterloo. He died in 1836 at the age of 28 and was buried with full military honours. The horse's gravestone can be seen under a large oak tree in the grounds.

HATFIELD HOUSE, HERTFORDSHIRE *below*

ELIZABETH I was given the news that she was to be the next Queen of England in the grounds of Hatfield House. The old Tudor palace where this event took place was demolished when the property passed to Robert Cecil, the first Earl of Salisbury, in 1603. He replaced it with the present Jacobean mansion which, in memory of the start of Elizabeth's reign, is shaped like a letter "E".

The house was altered over the years but most recent work has been directed towards restoring the Jacobean original. The great hall, the grand staircase, the armoury and long gallery are all characteristic of the period and have been painstakingly restored. The banqueting hall survives from Elizabeth's day and was the site of her first Council of State.

John Tradescant the Elder, the famous plant hunter, designed and laid out the gardens but his work was neglected when landscape gardening became the fashion in the 18th century. As with the house, the gardens are now being returned to their Jacobean layouts and include formal, knot, scented and wilderness areas.

CHARTWELL, KENT *below*

ATTRACTED BY THE EXTENSIVE views over The Weald and the South Downs, Sir Winston Churchill bought Chartwell in 1922 and lived there until his death in 1965. He made extensive additions and alterations to the original Victorian house.

Chartwell was very much a retreat and Churchill indulged in his hobbies of painting, writing and bricklaying during his time there. The house was purchased by a group of Churchill's friends in 1946 and given to the National Trust to be preserved as a memorial to Britain's wartime Prime Minister.

The rooms and gardens at Chartwell are kept as they were in Churchill's time. Daily papers are delivered and Churchill's cigars are in evidence. Displays relating to his life and works occupy many of the rooms and his paintings can be viewed in his garden studio.

HEVER CASTLE, KENT *right*

HEVER CASTLE is best known as the childhood home of Anne Boleyn (1507-1536). The central Tudor manor house was built by the Boleyn family around 1500 while the stone gatehouse and outer walls date from the 13th century. The whole building is surrounded by a double moat. King Henry VIII wooed Anne at Hever Castle but after marrying and then beheading her, he gave the castle to his fourth wife, Anne of Cleves.

William Waldorf Astor, the American millionaire, bought Hever in 1903 and made great efforts to restore it. Most of the interior is the result of Astor's work, as are the collections of art and antiques. Astor recreated the gardens at Hever between 1904 and 1908. These include the Italian garden, the rose garden, the maze and a 35-acre lake. The Italian garden contains Roman and Renaissance statuary and sculpture. A Tudor herb garden was added in 1994.

KNOLE, KENT *left*

THE ORIGINAL palace at Knole was built between 1456 and 1486 for the Archbishop of Canterbury. Four more archbishops lived there before Thomas Cranmer gave it to Henry VIII. In 1566 Queen Elizabeth I passed the house on to Thomas Sackville, 1st Earl of Dorset, whose descendants continue to live there.

The 1st Earl remodelled the house between 1603 and 1608, adding panelling and plasterwork in the Great Hall and installing the great staircase. The exterior of the house has not changed substantially since. The Earl also began a collection of furniture for which Knole continues to be famous.

During the Civil War the house was sacked but restoration was carried out shortly afterwards when the 5th Earl married Lady Frances Cranfield who brought furniture, tapestries and paintings from Copt Hall, her family home in Essex. The 6th Earl, as Lord Chamberlain to William III, had the right to any furnishings discarded from the royal palaces and was thus able to continue the family's collection.

Knole was the birthplace of Vita Sackville-West, and is said to have inspired her friend Virginia Wolfe's historical fantasy *Orlando*. Knole is set in a 1,000-acre deer park.

HOLKHAM HALL, NORFOLK *above*

HOLKHAM HALL was conceived by Thomas Coke, 1st Earl of Leicester, on his return from his Grand Tour of Europe. It reflects his appreciation of the Palladian style and was built, under the direction of the architect Matthew Brettingham, between 1734 and 1764. Unfortunately Thomas Coke died in 1759 and never saw his great project completed. The building has remained substantially unchanged since its completion with the exception of a vestibule on the north side and terraced gardens to the south, which were added during the 1850s.

Among the highlights of the building are the ceiling of the spectacular 50ft (15.25m) high Marble Hall (mostly constructed from alabaster) which is from a design by Inigo Jones and the opulent salon where paintings by Rubens, Van Dyke and many others are on display.

SOMERLEYTON HALL, SUFFOLK *right*

SOMERLEYTON HALL combines Italian, French and even Dutch elements into an extravagant earl Victorian mansion. It was the work of Sir Morton Peto, who rose from being a bricklayer to become one of the most successful building contractors in England. Work began in 1844 and was substantially completed by 1851. Unfortunately Sir Morton was forced to sell his dream house 10 years late following financial difficulties. The courtyard is dominated by a clock designed by Vulliamy and there is an Italianate Victorian *campanile* tower. The two wings that flank the courtyard are connected b an elaborately carved French Renaissance-style stone screen. The gable ends of the two wings incorporate the old Dutch gables of the original Hall.

The Hall was purchased by the Crossley family in 1863 and continues to be owned by them.

KENTWELL HALL,
SUFFOLK *left*

KENTWELL HALL was built by the Clopton family, who had grown rich in the wool trade, between about 1500 and 1550. It is an excellent example of Tudor domestic architecture and decorative brickwork. Although the interior has been "improved" on a number of occasions by subsequent owners the outside of the building remains virtually unchanged. The most extensive remodelling took place in the 1820s when the architect Thomas Hopper gave the interior a Gothic style. The house was used as a transit camp during the Second World War but by 1971, when it was bought by the present owners, Patrick and Judith Phillips, it was in a very poor state of repair.

The Phillips family have returned the Hall to earlier glories and pioneered re-enactments of everyday life at the Hall during the Tudor period and the Second World War.

SANDRINGHAM HOUSE, NORFOLK *above*

SANDRINGHAM HOUSE WAS BOUGHT by the Prince and Princess of Wales, later King Edward VII and Queen Alexandra, in 1862. The original Georgian structure had been completely remodelled by 1870 and continued to expand as the Prince's family grew. Only a serious fire in 1891 has marred its otherwise tranquil development.

The House continues to be a private retreat of the royal family, although the main ground floor rooms are open to the public when they are not in residence. The décor has changed little since the Edwardian period and there are extensive collections of objets d'art, many of which were gifts from visiting dignitaries.

The royal family usually spend Christmas at Sandringham and remain there officially until February. King George VI died at Sandringham in 1952.

OSBORNE HOUSE, ISLE OF WIGHT *below*

OSBORNE HOUSE WAS PURCHASED BY Queen Victoria and Prince Albert in 1845. Victoria knew the Isle of Wight from her childhood and wanted Osborne House as a summer retreat. Her original intention had been to embellish the original building but eventually it was demolished and replaced by the present Italianate villa. The grounds acquired a summer house, a Swiss cottage, a miniature fort and barracks and a museum.

One of the grandest rooms at Osborne House is the Durbar Room which commemorates Queen Victoria's role as Empress of India. It was built between 1890-91, for holding state receptions. The terrace gardens were designed by Cubitt and Prince Albert himself. They are in a formal Italianate style to match the house.

After the death of Prince Albert, Queen Victoria spent a great deal of time at Osborne and died there in 1901.

BEAULIEU, HAMPSHIRE *below*

BEAULIEU HOUSE BEGAN LIFE as the great gatehouse of Beaulieu Abbey and dates back to the 14th century. The abbey and its estates were purchased in 1538 by Sir Thomas Wrothesley, later 1st Earl of Southampton, on the Dissolution of the Monasteries.

The present building is largely the result of extensions by Lord Henry Scott in the 1870s. The architect, Sir Arthur Blomfield, created a mixture of Victorian Gothic, medieval Gothic and 18th-century fortification styles.

During the Second World War, Beaulieu was used as a training ground for secret agents and at least one member of the Montagu family operated as a spy herself in Nazi-occupied Europe.

The Beaulieu estate also houses the remains of the original 13th-century Cistercian abbey and the National Motor Museum.

LONGLEAT HOUSE AND GARDENS, WILTSHIRE *above*

JOHN THYNNE, THE BUILDER OF Longleat House, was a former clerk of the kitchens to Henry VIII who bought the estate for £53 in 1541. The house is Italianate in style and was completed in 1580 (the year Thynne died). It received the first of many royal visitors, Queen Elizabeth I, in 1574 and is now the home of the Marquises of Bath. The 4th Marquis of Bath took the unusual step of employing Italian craftsmen to make the internal decorations and the furniture match the exterior.

The gardens were landscaped in the 18th century by Capability Brown. He was responsible for the formal gardens, the orangery, and the terraces. The present Marquess of Bath converted the inner part of the estate into a wildlife park.

WILTON HOUSE, WILTSHIRE *right*

WILTON HOUSE stands on land acquired by the Earls of Pembroke from Henry VIII in 1542 but the current Palladian-style building dates from the 17th century and is attributed to Inigo Jones. Work to improve the estate of Wilton began in 1632 when Isaac De Caus initiated a project to transform the gardens with water features stretching over 300 yards across the river. Plans were also drawn up to extend the house but these had to be scaled down due to the Civil War and lack of funds. The house was not completed until the middle of the 17th century.

The most spectacular aspect of the interior is the Double Cube Room which is 60ft (18.25m) long by 30ft (9m) wide and 30ft (9m) high. Designed by Inigo Jones it is believed to be the finest surviving example of a mid 17th-century room in England.

✳

TYNTESFIELD, SOMERSET *below*

WILLIAM GIBBS, the man who transformed a modest country house called Tyntes Place into today's Tyntesfield, made his fortune importing guano (seabird droppings) into Britain from South America. In the mid 19th century guano was Britain's most popular garden fertiliser.

Gibbs bought his house in 1843 and employed the architect John Norton to rebuild it as a Gothic Revival extravaganza. Towers and turrets were added to the building while land was added to the garden. The original Victorian interiors have changed little and Tyntesfield possesses an excellent collection of Victorian decorative art. A highlight is the richly decorated private chapel. The grounds include formal gardens and a walled kitchen as well as more open parkland. Tyntesfield was bought by the National Trust in 2002 after a successful campaign to preserve it.

STANWAY HOUSE, GLOUCESTERSHIRE *above*

STANWAY IS A JACOBEAN MANOR HOUSE completed in the 1630s in Cotswold stone and local slate. Its owners, the Tracy family and their descendants, the Earls of Wemyss, claim descent from the emperor Charlemagne. Other buildings on the site include a fine gatehouse, a church and a 14th-century tithe barn. Much of the furniture, such as the working Charles I shuffleboard table, is original to the house.

The most unusual feature of Stanway is its 18th-century water-garden. This was probably designed by the landscape gardener Charles Bridgeman and includes a formal canal on a terrace above the house, the longest cascade in England, a pyramid and a further eight ponds. Many of these features have been reinstated in the last 10 years and a 165ft (50.2m) single-jet fountain has been added.

BLENHEIM PALACE, OXFORDSHIRE *above*

BLENHEIM PALACE was presented to John Churchill, the first Duke of Marlborough, as a reward for his victory over the French at Blenheim in 1704. It was to have been paid for by Queen Anne but, due to political intrigue, the money never arrived and the work was finally completed in 1722 at the Duke's expense.

Designed by Sir John Vanbrugh and Nicholas Hawksmoor, Blenheim Palace is the supreme example of English Baroque architecture with carvings by Grinling Gibbons and a painting, by Sir James Thornhill, of the Battle of Blenheim on the 67ft (20.4m) high ceiling of the Great Hall. The building is adorned with family portraits by artists such as Keller, Romney, Reynolds, Sargent and Van Dyck. The gardens were originally laid out by Capability Brown but have been modified and added to over the years. Winston Churchill was born at Blenheim Palace on November 30, 1874. He also proposed to his wife there and is buried close by.

COTTESBROOKE HALL, NORTHAMPTONSHIRE *right*

COTTESBROOKE HALL, which dates from 1702, is a fine example of Queen Anne architect although it is not known who designed it. Some improvements were made during the late 1 century, including east and west bows in the Adam manner and a bridge built by Robert Mitchel 1765. The interior of the house features some very unusual papier mâché rococo wall decoration

The Hall is said to be the inspiration for Mansfield Park in Jane Austen's novel of that name. To it houses collections of furniture and porcelain as well as the Woolavington Collection of spor paintings. This includes works by Stubbs, Marshall and many others.

Although the park was landscaped in the 18th century the gardens were principally develope the 20th century in a style inspired by the Arts and Crafts movement with geometric beds and a cl boundary between house and garden.

CHARLECOTE PARK, WARWICKSHIRE *right*

PARTS OF CHARLECOTE PARK date back to 1551, although most of the exterior is from the 19th century when extensive restoration work was carried out. It has been the home of the Lucy family since the 12th century. The interior of the house contains many curiosities collected by the family over the years.

The gatehouse is wholly original and features the arms of Queen Elizabeth I in commemoration of her two-day visit in 1572. Other visitors have included Lord Nelson and Queen Victoria. William Shakespeare is said to have been caught poaching deer in the grounds and to have lampooned the then owner of Charlecote, Sir Thomas Lucy, as Justice Shallow in The Merry Wives of Windsor.

The park was landscaped by the indefatigable Capability Brown.

✳

ALTHORP PARK, NORTHAMPTONSHIRE *left*

SIR JOHN SPENCER erected a house at Althorp at the beginning of the 16th century. It had an enclosed courtyard with projecting wings on the south side but in 1660-62 the courtyard was roofed in and a grand staircase installed. The red brick façade was "classicised" by the Second Earl of Sunderland; columns were added; a balustrade placed on the elevation; the great hall transformed into a long gallery and the gardens were redesigned by Le Nôtre who had previously worked at Versailles.

After some years of neglect, the house was given a French neo-classical makeover by Henry Holland at the end of the 18th century. The walls were covered in precision-fitting "mathematical" tiles; pediments were added to the north and south fronts; and new stone dressings to the front entrance. The roof was also lowered, and the chimneys reconstructed. The house exterior has not changed substantially since.

Althorp is best known today as the childhood home of Diana, Princess of Wales, and now houses an exhibition in her honour.

CHATSWORTH, DERBYSHIRE *left*

THE FIRST HOUSE AT CHATSWORTH was built in the late 1500s by the redoubtable Elizabethan matriarch Bess of Hardwick and the second of her four husbands Sir William Cavendish. The Hunting Tower, on the hill behind Chatsworth, is all that remains from this period. Bess's last husband was the custodian of Mary Queen of Scots, who was imprisoned from time to time at Chatsworth.

The current building was started in the 1690s, beginning with new family rooms, the State Apartments, the East Front, the Painted Hall and a long gallery. A grand formal garden was designed and the famous Cascade was constructed. By 1707 Chatsworth had been almost completely rebuilt and it has been little altered since.

The original formal gardens were later remodelled by Capability Brown in the late 18th century to give the park a more natural, romantic look but the gardens that exist today were not commissioned until 1826. Plants were collected from all over world, rockeries were built and a "Conservative Wall" glasshouse constructed. In charge of the work was Joseph Paxton who also designed the Emperor Fountain which has a jet that can reach over 280 feet (85 metres).

HARDWICK HALL, DERBYSHIRE *above*

NOT ONLY WAS BESS OF HARDWICK the inspiration behind Chatsworth, she was also the moving force behind Derbyshire's other great stately home, Hardwick Hall. She was the second richest woman in England during the reign of Elizabeth I. She had four husbands and founded the Cavendish dynasty. She was born in Hardwick Old Hall (now a ruin on the estate) and commissioned Robert Smythson, the architect of Longleat, to build the new hall in 1590. Work was finished in 1597 and, remarkably, the house has changed little since.

The house, standing on a rise that dominates its surroundings, is a basic rectangle with projecting towers on the corners and two of the sides. The numerous windows give an otherwise very solid house an insubstantial appearance. "ES" crests identify the property as that of Elizabeth of Shrewsbury, Bess's official title.

The inside of the Hall is as well preserved as the outside and contains outstanding collections of 16th-century embroidery, tapestries, furniture and portraits. The grounds contain herb gardens, walled gardens, orchards and a park.

CHOLMONDELEY CASTLE, CHESHIRE *below*

THE CHOLMONDELEY (pronounced "Chumley") family dates back to the time of William the Conqueror and they have been prominent landholders in Cheshire since at least the 13th century. The present castle was built between 1801 and 1804 by the 4th Earl of Cholmondeley (later the 1st Marquess). It stands on a high rise above a lake and is an excellent early example of Gothic revivalism.

The castle remains a private family home but the extensive gardens are open to the public. These include a temple water garden, a rose garden and a silver garden containing distinctive silver-leafed plants in commemoration of the Queen's Silver Jubilee in 1977.

TATTON HALL, CHESHIRE *right*

TATTON HALL was started in 1790 as a replacement for an original brick building. William Egerton commissioned Samuel Wyatt to build an extensive neo-classical design; the first phase was completed in 1791. After a gap of 17 years and the death of Samuel, his nephew, Lewis Wyatt scaled down the original plans to complete the present mansion.

The neo-classical portico leads into various well-appointed state rooms, most notably the dining, music and drawing rooms, and a particularly fine library built to house the Egerton's collection of over 12,000 books. Paintings by Chardin, Canaletto, Nazari and Van Dyck are on display.

HOGHTON TOWER, LANCASHIRE *right*

HOGHTON TOWER began life as a medieval pele tower but was almost entirely reconstructed by Thomas Hoghton during the Elizabethan period. The Banqueting Hall is said to be the place where James I dubbed a side of beef "Sirloin" in August 1617. The house still contains a bedchamber, audience chamber and ballroom used by King James. There is rather more evidence that a young William Shakespeare spent some time at Hoghton. The tower was besieged for about a week by Parliamentary troops in February 1643 but when the attackers entered the house, the powder magazine in the pele tower exploded, killing over 100 men and causing extensive damage. The central tower was never rebuilt.

The house, restored in its original style, continued to welcome royal guests including William III, George V and Queen Mary, and the Duke of Edinburgh. It is still the home of the de Hoghton family.

CASTELL COCH, CARDIFF *left*

ASTELL COCH, OR "RED CASTLE", takes its name from the red sandstone of the original castle
hat stood on this site. During the 13th century the Norman de Clare family probably added a small
val courtyard and three circular towers to a pre-existing stone castle. However this building seems
o have been abandoned early in the 14th century and, by the 19th century, it was little more than
picturesque ruin.

The present castle is almost entirely the creation of the 3rd Marquis of Bute, a rich and eccentric
ictorian plutocrat. Work began in 1875 under the supervision of William Burges to create a
elatively authentic reconstruction of a medieval castle which also happens to be a comfortable
amily home. Attention to historical detail did not extend to the interiors which are wonderful
xamples of high Victorian fantasy.

FONMON CASTLE, VALE OF GLAMORGAN *above*

THE RECTANGULAR KEEP at Fonmon Castle was built around 1200 and one of its surviving
towers is also from the medieval period. Originally built by the St John family, the castle was
purchased from them by the ancestor of the present owners during the English Civil War.

The present building has developed largely by the addition of wings to existing buildings but it
does feature some exceptional Georgian interiors. The castle remains a private family home but
many areas including the gardens, the hall, the drawing room, the library, and the kitchen are open
to visitors.

Fonmon has been the family home of the Boothbys since the middle of the 17th century and
Clara, Lady Boothby (1854-1946) the first president of the Fuchsia Society, lived at Fonmon Castle.

CASTLE HOWARD, YORKSHIRE *above*

WHEN JOHN VANBRUGH was asked to design Castle Howard by the 3rd Earl of Carlisle in 1699 he was known only as a dramatist and had never built anything in his life.

However, with the assistance of Nicholas Hawksmoor, he rose to the challenge and by the time of his death in 1726 two-thirds of this magnificent Baroque building had been completed. At the centre of the building was a striking masonry dome, the first used on a private residence in England. The facades were elaborately and ornately carved but the pilasters on the two fronts did not match; the north front had Doric columns and the south had Corinthian. Hawksmoor merely observed that nobody could see both fronts simultaneously.

Vanbrugh's designs were never completed and the west wing of the house is in a much plainer Palladian style. In 1940 fire broke out and destroyed the dome and nearly 20 rooms. The dome has since been rebuilt and redecorated. Castle Howard came to the attention of the public when it was used for the filming of *Brideshead Revisited*.

NEWBY HALL, YORKSHIRE *right*

THE MAIN BLOCK OF NEWBY HALL was built in the 1690s in the style of Sir Christopher Wren. It was bought in 1748 by the Weddell family and considerably extended by William Weddell in the 1760s. Weddell wanted somewhere to house the treasures he had brought back from his Grand Tour and commissioned John Carr to add two new wings to the Hall. In 1767 Robert Adam was asked to complete the work with his customary elegance. The Adam rooms now display Weddell's collection of classical sculpture and his set of Gobelin tapestries.

The 3rd Lord Grantham inherited the Hall in 1792 and decided to change Adam's south-facing dining room into a library and build a new dining room on the north-west corner of the house. Grantham designed these rooms himself. A further wing was added during the Victorian period which is at odds with the elegance of the rest of the house. The gardens were planned and developed in the 20th century.

HOLKER HALL, CUMBRIA

left

HOLKER HALL is a combination of Elizabethan, neo-classical and Gothic styles. The oldest parts date from the late 16th century but the east and north wings were added after 1756 under the supervision of John Carr of York. The gardens were also landscaped at this time.

William the 2nd Earl of Burlington completely renovated Holker between 1838 and 1842. Ornamental chimneys and windows were grafted on to the house to make it more Gothic, while stables, a conservatory and larger gardens were added to the grounds. Unfortunately a fire in 1871 destroyed most of the West Wing. The restoration of the West Wing completed the building's development.

The library at Holker Hall houses a collection of over 3,500 books, and includes works by the 18th century scientist Henry Cavendish. The Hall is still owned by the Cavendish family. The 25-acre gardens have won many national awards.

HAREWOOD HOUSE, YORKSHIRE *left*

BEGUN IN 1759, HAREWOOD HOUSE was designed by John Carr and features interiors by Robert Adam. The neo-classical building is over 248 ft (75.5 m) long and 84 ft (25.6 m) wide and consists of a centre and two wings in Corinthian style. Adam's superb ceilings and plasterwork can still be seen as can much of the original furniture designed for the house by Chippendale. The good taste of the 18th century is also demonstrated by the extensive collection of English and Italian paintings.

The grounds were landscaped by Capability Brown and feature lakeside and woodland walks as well as an intricate parterre terrace designed by Sir Charles Barry.

The house is home to the Earl of Harewood who is a cousin of HM Queen Elizabeth II.

BELSAY HALL, NORTHUMBERLAND *below*

BELSAY HALL WAS DESIGNED in 1807 by Sir Charles Monck in an attempt to blend Greek Revival style with a modern country house. It is said to have been inspired by the Temple of Theseus in Athens. After falling into some disrepair it has been substantially restored in recent years with the replacement of missing floors and the opening up of many formerly disused rooms. Near the Hall is a medieval castle consisting of a tower house and a Jacobean manor, added in 1614.

The impressive Quarry Garden was also designed by Sir Charles Monck. Listed as Grade I in the Register of Parks and Gardens, it contains ravines, corridors and pinnacles as the setting for rare and exotic plants.

PALACE OF HOLYROOD HOUSE, EDINBURGH *above*

SCOTTISH KINGS HAVE lived at Holyrood since the 12th century when David I founded a monastery there. A number of buildings have stood on the site but the present one owes much to Charles II who repaired and remodelled it after it had been extensively damaged during the Civil War. He added royal apartments, converted the Abbey Church into the Chapel Royal and created extensive and generously proportioned accommodation on the second floor for the use of the Court. On the exterior, mainly classical facades were built round a central quadrangle.

After the Act of Union, Holyrood became the haunt of distressed noblemen living in "grace-and-favour" apartments, but some excitement returned in 1745 when Bonnie Prince Charlie briefly held court there. The roof of the Abbey Church collapsed in 1768, leaving the Chapel Royal in ruins.

George IV's state visit to Scotland in 1822 changed the palace's fortunes for the better. Restoration began, and the apartments of Mary, Queen of Scots were ordered to be preserved. Queen Victoria continued to favour Holyrood House and it has remained popular with the royal family ever since.

✳

LINLITHGOW PALACE, EDINBURGH *right*

LINLITHGOW PALACE is best-known as the birthplace of Mary Queen of Scots. The ruins that can be seen today date back to 1424 when King James I began a royal residence there. Over the next 200 years the building was transformed into a palace that was comparable to any of the great houses of Europe.

The palace began to fall into disrepair after Mary Queen of Scots' brief personal reign, but occasional renovations and improvements, including the fine Renaissance façade of the north range, took place until the reign of Charles I. In 1745 Bonnie Prince Charlie became the last Stuart to stay at Linlithgow. In 1746 occupying troops set fires that burnt the building out.

Since then the palace has remained deserted and unroofed, though some attempts have been made to stop its decay beginning, in 1906, with the restoration of the fireplace in the great hall.

SCONE PALACE, PERTHSHIRE *above*

SCONE WAS ORIGINALLY the site of a sixth-century Celtic church which was replaced in the 12th century by an Augustinian abbey and a bishop's palace. The kings of Scotland traditionally lodged at the palace before they were crowned. Both the palace and abbey were destroyed in 1559 by a Perth mob, incited by the preacher John Knox.

In 1604 the Scone estates were given to Sir David Murray who built a new palace there in 1618. Charles II stayed in this palace before becoming the last King crowned at Scone. Murray's descendants eventually became Earls of Mansfield. The 3rd Earl, David Murray, commissioned the rebuilding of the palace as the splendid castellated Tudor Gothic edifice in red sandstone that can be seen today. The architect was William Atkinson, who went on to create Abbotsford in the Scottish Borders for Sir Walter Scott.

First published in 2010 by Myriad Books Limited
35 Bishopsthorpe Road, London SE26 4PA

www. myriadbooks.co.uk

Text copyright © John Mannion
John Mannion has asserted his right under the Copyright, Designs and Patents Act 1998 to be identified as the author of this work.

ISBN 1 847 46 343 6
EAN 978 1 84746 343 2

Designed by Jerry Goldie
Printed in China

All of the photographs in this book have be supplied by Skyscan Photolibrary. Skysc have been involved in aerial photograp since 1984, taking and organising new pho graphic projects as well as running photolibrary of stock aerial images. Th represent the work of many aerial a aviation photographers worldwide as w as their own Skyscan™ Balloon Came collection of British towns and landscap Further information can be found on the website www.Skyscan.co.uk

All photographs are copyright Skyscan ap from the following which were captured associates and contributing photographers the Skyscan Photolibrary: 2 (top), 4 (top a bottom), 5, 9 (bottom), 20 (top), Flig Images; 12, D Wootton;16 (bottom), B Eva 28 (top), W Cross; 21, I Bracegirdle; K Whitcombe; 31, 32, R West.